LET'S DRAW KOOKY CHARACTERS WITH CRAYOLA!

ILLUSTRATED BY CLAIRE STAMPER

LERNER PUBLICATIONS ◆ MINNEAPOLIS

Copyright © 2019 by Lerner Publishing Group, Inc.

All rights reserved. International copyright secured. No part of this book may be reproduced, stored in a retrieval system, or transmitted in any form or by any means—electronic, mechanical, photocopying, recording, or otherwise—without the prior written permission of Lerner Publishing Group, Inc., except for the inclusion of brief quotations in an acknowledged review.

© 2019 Crayola, Easton, PA 18044-0431. Crayola Oval Logo, Crayola, Serpentine Design, Pink Sherbert, Jazzberry Jam, and Purple Mountains' Majesty are registered trademarks of Crayola used under license.

Official Licensed Product
Lerner Publications Company
A division of Lerner Publishing Group, Inc.
241 First Avenue North
Minneapolis, MN 55401 USA

For reading levels and more information, look up this title at www.lernerbooks.com.

Main body text set in Billy Infant Regular.
Typeface provided by SparkyType.

Library of Congress Cataloging-in-Publication Data

Names: Stamper, Claire, 1990- illustrator.
Title: Let's draw kooky characters with Crayola! / illustrated by Claire Stamper.
Description: Minneapolis : Lerner Publications, 2019. | Series: Let's draw with Crayola! | Includes bibliographical references. | Audience: Ages 4-9. | Audience: K to Grade 3.
Identifiers: LCCN 2018006138 (print) | LCCN 2018016011 (ebook) | ISBN 9781541512566 (eb pdf) | ISBN 9781541511040 (lb : alk. paper)
Subjects: LCSH: Characters and characteristics in art—Juvenile literature. | Drawing—Technique—Juvenile literature.
Classification: LCC NC825.C43 (ebook) | LCC NC825.C43 L48 2019 (print) | DDC 741.2—dc23

LC record available at https://lccn.loc.gov/2018006138

Manufactured in the United States of America
1-43993-34002-8/10/2018

CONTENTS

Can You Draw Kooky Characters? . . 4
Pirates and Mermaids 6
Ninjas 8
Fairies and Leprechauns 10
Unicorns 12
Wizards and Witches 14
Superheroes 16
Circus Performers 18
Cowboys and Cowgirls 20
Farmer and Scarecrow 22
Cops and Robbers 24
Mad Scientists 26
Kooky Character School 28

World of Colors 30
To Learn More 32

CAN YOU DRAW KOOKY CHARACTERS?

You can if you can draw shapes! Use the shapes in the box at the top of each page to draw the character parts. Put the parts together in your drawing to make a sneaky ninja or a beautiful mermaid. Or use the parts to make your own character!

CHARACTER PARTS

Shapes you will use: triangle, circle, rectangle, half circle, oval, square

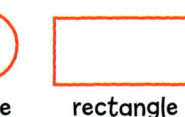

Hats

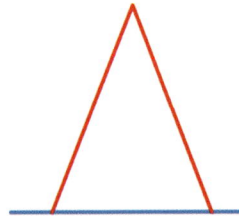

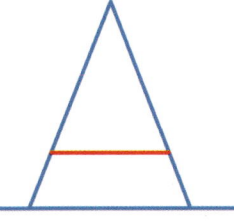

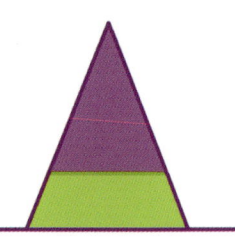

4

Eyes and Noses

Accessories

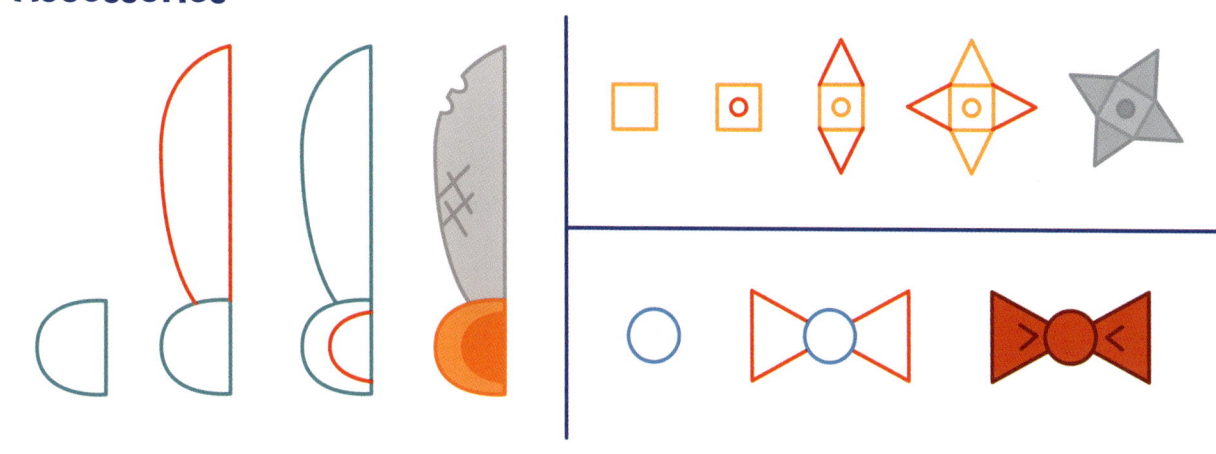

Hands

5

PIRATES AND MERMAIDS

Shapes you will use:
circle, half circle, triangle, trapezoid, rectangle, oval

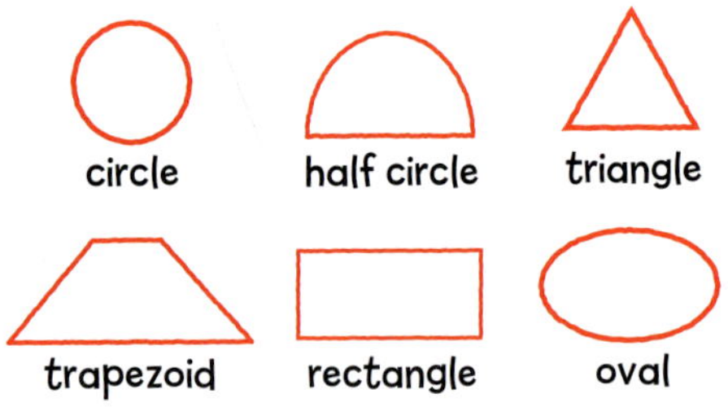

Captain Beardy

Melinda Mermaid

6

Pirate Penny

Pinky

7

Shapes you will use:

- circle
- half circle
- triangle
- trapezoid
- rectangle
- oval

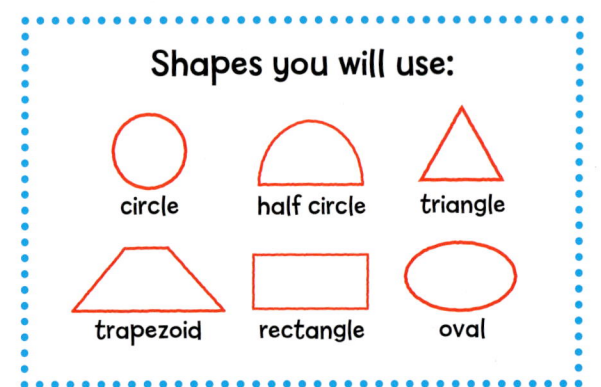

Sneaky

8

Throwing Starr

Ninja Nick

9

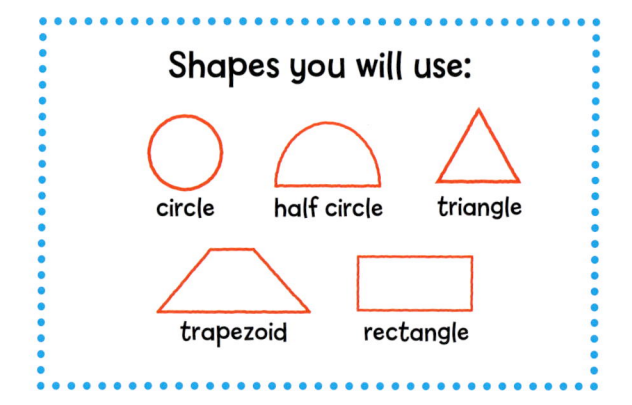

Shapes you will use:

- circle
- half circle
- triangle
- trapezoid
- rectangle

FAIRIES AND LEPRECHAUNS

Sunny

10

Violet

Mickey

11

UNICORNS

Shapes you will use:

- circle
- half circle
- triangle
- trapezoid
- rectangle
- oval

Sparkles

12

Cotton Candy

13

WIZARDS AND WITCHES

Shapes you will use:
- circle
- half circle
- triangle
- trapezoid
- square
- oval

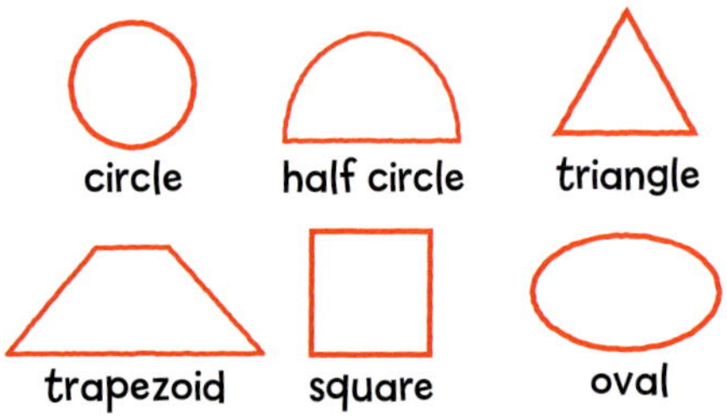

Wanda

Magical Marv

Wiz Kid

15

SUPERHEROES

Shapes you will use:
- circle
- half circle
- triangle
- trapezoid
- rectangle
- oval

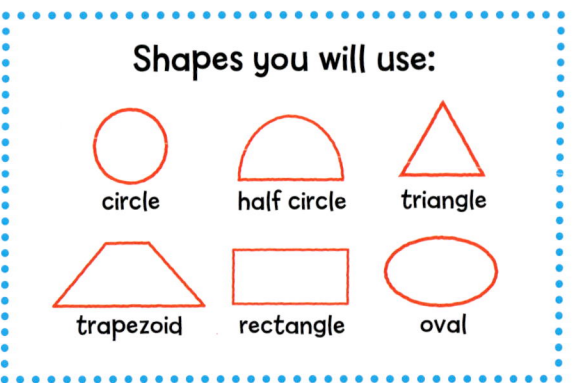

Flying Fiona

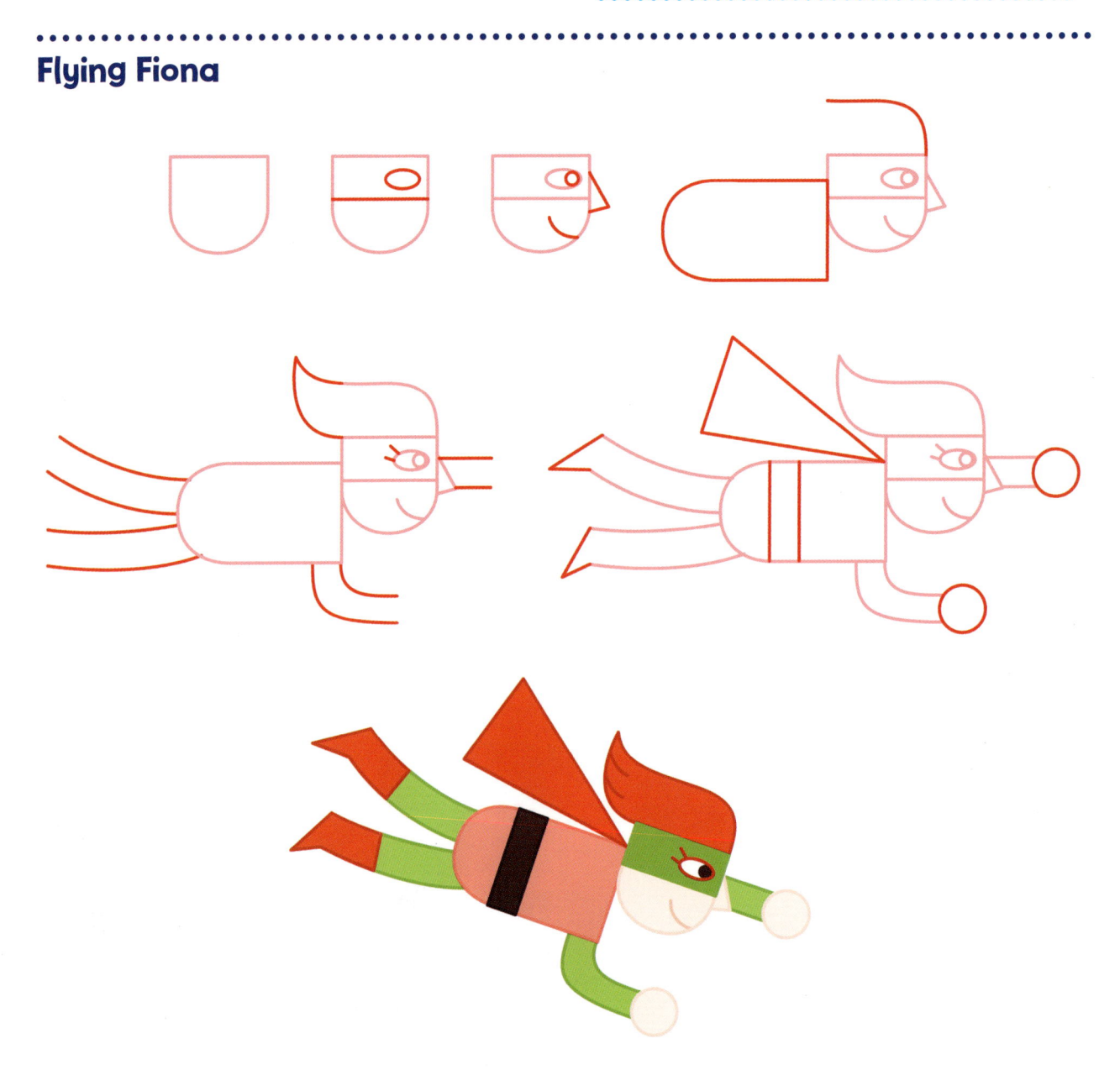

16

Super Cat

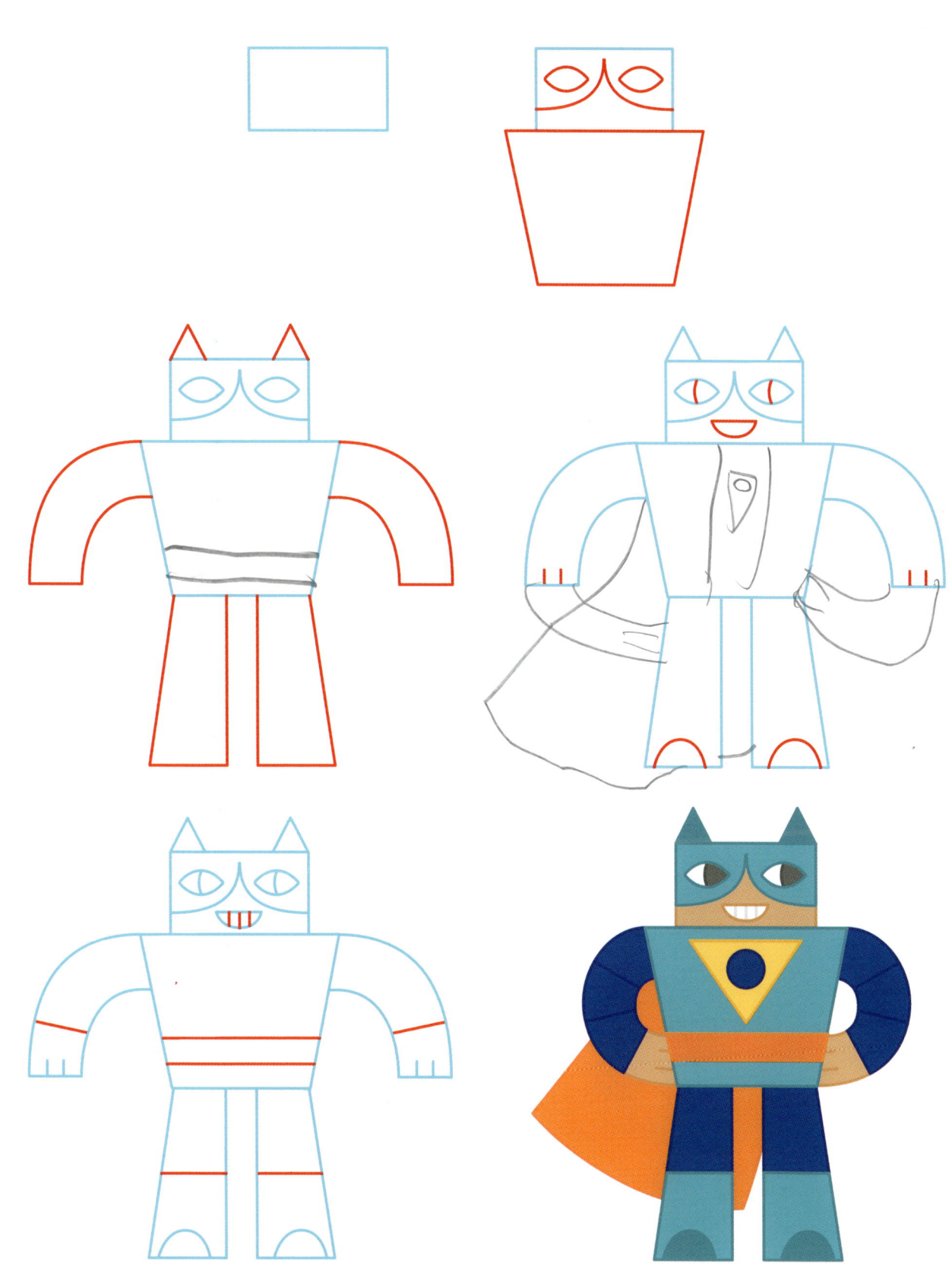

CIRCUS PERFORMERS

Shapes you will use:
- circle
- half circle
- triangle
- trapezoid
- rectangle

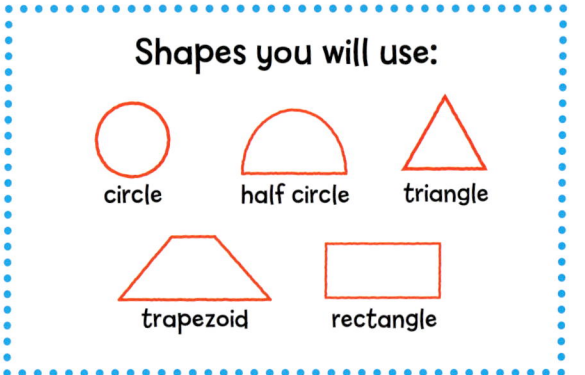

The Grand Master

18

Ana the Acrobat

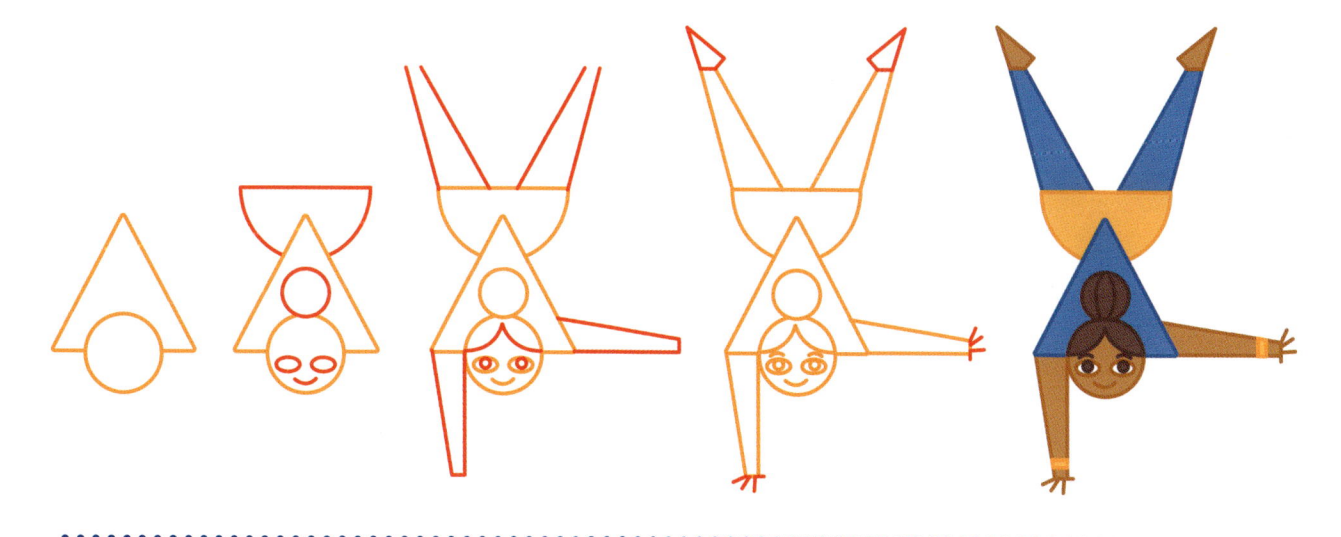

Super Strong Saul

19

COWBOYS AND COWGIRLS

Shapes you will use:
circle, half circle, triangle, trapezoid, rectangle, oval

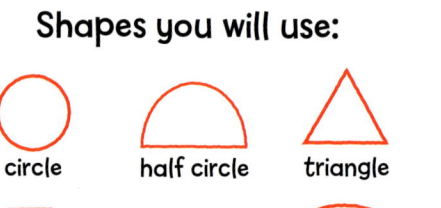

Rowdy Ron

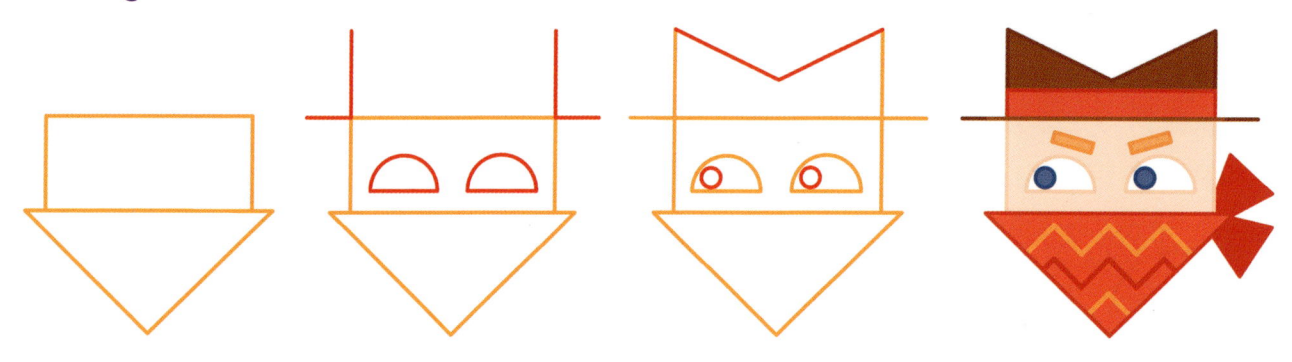

Wild West Willy

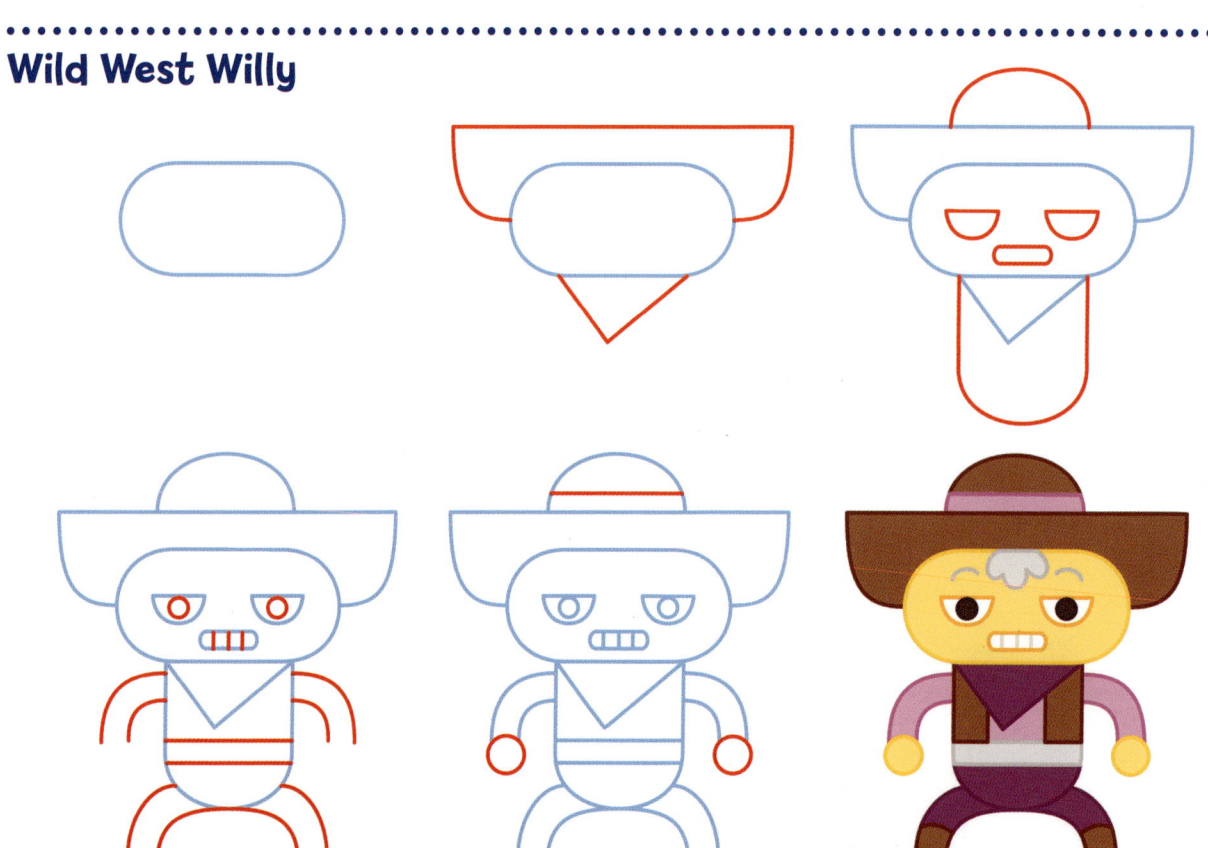

20

Cowgirl Callie

21

FARMER AND SCARECROW

Shapes you will use:
- circle
- half circle
- triangle
- trapezoid
- rectangle
- square

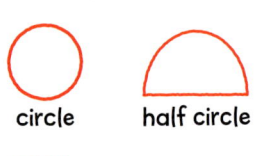

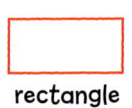

Friendly Scarecrow

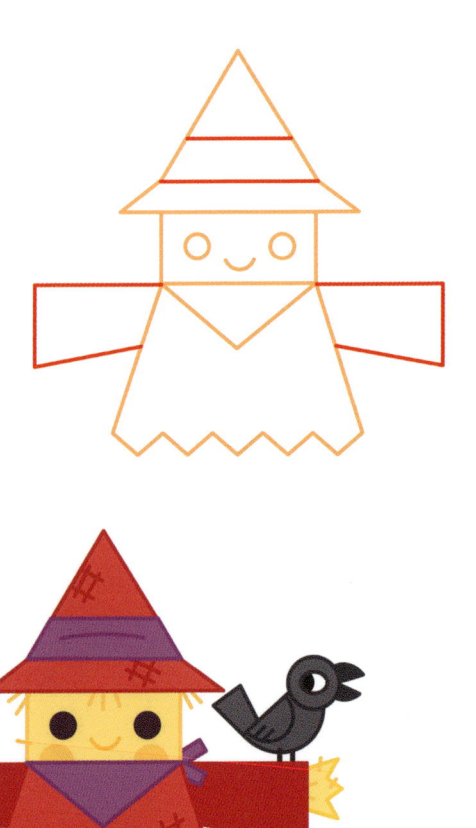

22

Farmer Fred

23

COPS AND ROBBERS

Shapes you will use:
circle, half circle, triangle, square, trapezoid, rectangle, oval

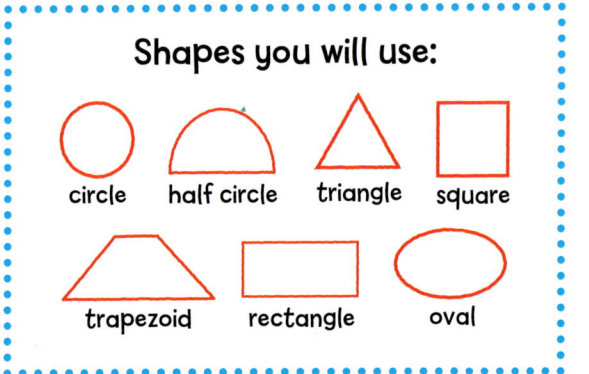

Stripes

Copper

24

Robber Roberta

Officer Olaf

25

MAD SCIENTISTS

Shapes you will use:
- trapezoid
- rectangle
- half circle
- circle
- oval
- triangle

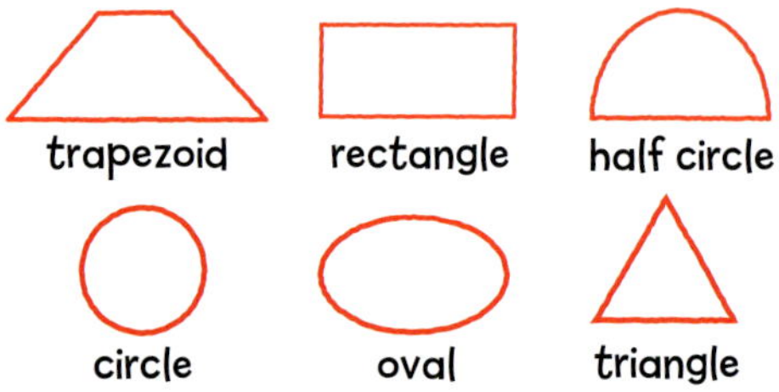

Specs

26

The Professor

KOOKY CHARACTER SCHOOL

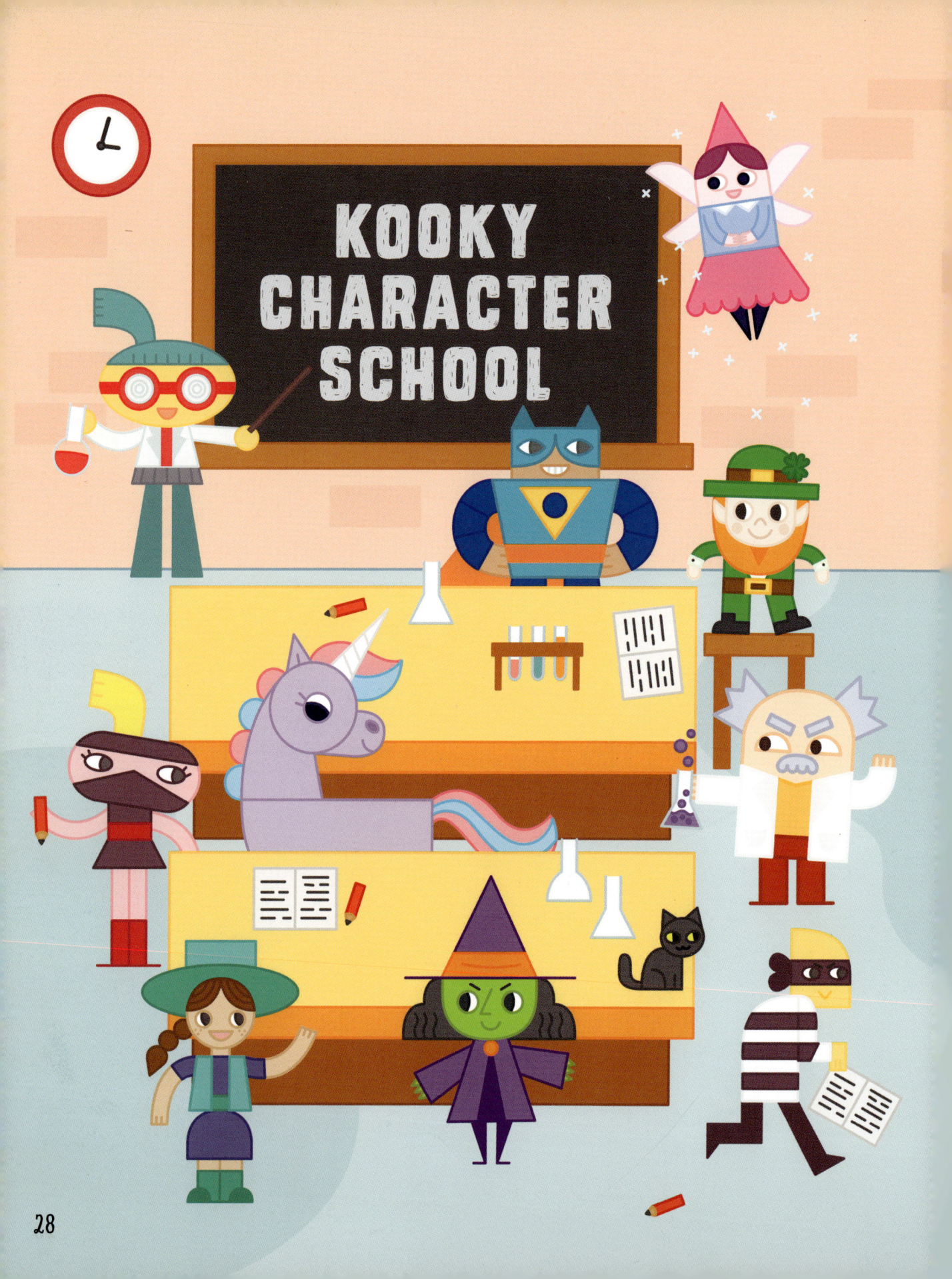

29

WORLD OF COLORS

There are kooky colors all around us! Here are some of the Crayola® crayon colors used in this book. What colors will you use to draw your next character?

SEPIA | PINK SHERBERT | JAZZBERRY JAM | BRICK RED | RED | PEACH | YELLOW ORANGE | DANDELION | YELLOW

YEE-HAW! DRAW!

- YELLOW GREEN
- SHAMROCK
- GREEN
- AQUAMARINE
- SKY BLUE
- NAVY BLUE
- MIDNIGHT BLUE
- BLUE VIOLET
- PURPLE MOUNTAINS' MAJESTY

TO LEARN MORE

Books

Garbot, Dave. *Crazy, Zany Cartoon Characters.* Irvine, CA: Walter Foster Jr., 2015.
Take a look at this book to learn how to draw even more hilarious characters.

Legendre, Philippe. *Princesses, Fairies & Fairy Tales: Learn to Draw Pretty Princesses and Fairy Tale Characters Step by Step!* Irvine, CA: Walter Foster Jr., 2015.
Check out this book to learn to draw more fairy-tale creatures such as fairies, mermaids, and dragons.

Let's Draw Monsters with Crayola! Illustrated by Susanna Rumiz. Minneapolis: Lerner Publications, 2018.
Looking to draw other characters? Learn how to draw monsters in this book.

Websites

Comic Strip Capers
http://www.crayola.com/crafts/comic-strip-capers-craft/
Tell a story with your kooky characters! Visit this website to learn how to create your own comic strip.

How to Draw Fairy Tales
http://www.hellokids.com/r_580/drawing-for-kids/drawing-lessons-for-kids/how-to-draw-fairy-tales
Check out this website to get more practice drawing your favorite fairy-tale characters.